The Book of TAROT

The Book of TAROT

Illustrated with the Morgan-Greer Tarot

By Susan Gerulskis-Estes

U.S. GAMES SYSTEMS, INC.
Publishers • Stamford, CT
06902 USA

U.S. Games Systems, Inc.
Publishers • 179 Ludlow Street Stamford, CT
06902 USA

International Standard Book Number 0-88079-277-9

Printed in the United States of America

Contents

Preface 7

Origin of the Tarot 9

Structure 13

Kabalah and the Suits 15

Numerology and the Tarot 19

The Major Arcana 21

The Minor Arcana 51

Storage of the Cards 85

Reading the Cards 86

The Ancient Celtic Method of Divination 87

Astrological Readings 90

European Method 93

Meditation and the Tarot 94

Bibliography 95

THE WORLD

I saw eternity the other night
Like a great ring of pure and endless light
All calm, as it was bright
And round beneath it, time in hours, days, years
Driven by the spheres
Like a vast shadow moved; in which the
world
And all her train were hurled

Henry Vaughan
1621–1695

Preface

Conscious thought and meditation upon the Tarot over the centuries have caused the Tarot to exist as a very powerful entity. It has survived through the ages from so distant a past that no one can accurately trace its origin. There is a real presence of power behind the magical images of the Tarot. When using the Tarot cards one is in actuality invoking the state of one's being. Therefore, the Tarot is not to be taken lightly.

From its earliest creation, the Tarot was drawn with highly psychic images meant to provoke particular thoughts and feelings for the viewer to explore. These psychic images include universal symbols that have been built up in strength over the years through contemplation and meditation. Meditation acknowledges and develops the entity each card represents, thus causing its greater existence. For example, each time a person acknowledges and then meditates upon a symbol, the very fact that the person is meditating upon it causes its being. Continued acknowledgment and meditation reinforces the entity. Different thoughts will add or detract from the original concept of the image, which will cause it to grow or wither in its own development. But, nevertheless, it does exist.

The idea of the Tarot is subjective to the individual personality. Some oppose the Tarot; certain religious organizations consider the cards sacrilegious and condemn their use.

Throughout history there has been much religious opposition to using cards of any sort, including the Tarot. In 1378, cards in general were banned in Regensburg, Germany. Somewhere between 1450–70 in Italy, a Franciscan friar condemned dice and cards including the twenty-two cards of the Major Arcana.

The Tarot is certainly not sacrilegious and it is a lack of knowledge of the Tarot that causes such harsh judgment.

Anything that falls into the wrong hands can be used in a negative way, such as a knife, but one could certainly not condemn the use of a knife. A knife can be destructive but if used in a positive way, it becomes a very helpful and necessary tool. So with the Tarot. The Tarot contains knowledge that is eternal, therefore invaluable. There is no limit to the extent of the wisdom contained in the cards. What they reveal about this life, the before-life, the afterlife, the whole of nature, cause and effect, and the paths of existence, is remarkable. When a person fears or condemns the Tarot, one wonders what is really being feared or condemned.

The Tarot is an entity meant to be taken seriously. Using the Tarot for games of entertainment is not their correct or intended use. People who use them as such will, hopefully, lose interest in them.

Divination is the art of revealing what is in one's mind, conscious or subconscious, and the probability of future events through the cards. The person who foretells events or reads the cards is referred to as the Diviner and the person who searches for answers is referred to as the Seeker. Divination increases awareness and develops intuition. It also brings one to a better understanding of one's position in the universe.

Fortune-telling for its own sake or for amusement is another form of misuse of the Tarot. However, foretelling probable events based upon the knowledge of the Tarot for the sincere purpose of examining one's life and direction is a noble use of the cards. Divination will develop intuition and ease spiritual development into daily life if done properly. Readings should be used to analyze and understand situations so that they can be improved.

ORigin of the Tarot

The origin of the Tarot cards is surrounded by mystery. However, there are interesting theories about their creation, each extremely different and unrelated.

One theory propounds that the Tarot was invented by prehistoric man for use as a calendar noting nature's cycles.

Another theory suggests an artist named Jacquemin Gringonneur invented the deck for the amusement of Charles VI of France.

Antoine Court de Gebelin wrote in 1392 that the Tarot was actually a book saved from one of the temples of Egypt, when all other writings were destroyed by fire. He believed the Tarot cards were the remains of The Book of Thoth, Lord of Magic. Thoth, the Egyptian god of wisdom, occult knowledge, and the arts and sciences, was also secretary to other gods in the Egyptian pantheon. The invention of numbers and sacred writings were both attributed to Thoth. He is often depicted with a man's body and the head and neck of an ibis and often carrying a tablet, pen, and palm branch. The Book of Thoth, written in hieroglyphics, and also referred to as the Book of Tarot, is supposed to have contained all wisdom and occult knowledge.

The Greeks gave Thoth the name Hermes Trismegitus and referred to his sacred abstruse works as Hermetic.

The twenty-two pictures of the Major Arcana were painted on the walls of an Egyptian initiation chamber located in the lower chambers of the Sphinx. To be initiated into the order of Hermes Thoth, the neophyte was taken through the gallery by a member of the order who would explain the symbolic meaning of the twenty-two pictures. The aspirant had to realize and understand the meaning of the pictures in order to gain enough courage, strength, and knowledge to complete the initiation. If the neophyte failed any of the initiation tests, he would be put to death.

Another theory states that the cards originated in India. The androgynous figure of the Hindu god Ardhanari contains in its four arms objects similar to those which represent the four suits of the Tarot. The objects to the right of Ardhanari, which is called Siva for its female form, resemble the staff and cup. On the left side is Siva's consort Devi, the male half, who holds a sword and a ring.

Hanuman, the monkey god, is also depicted bearing the same objects.

Vishnu, the god known as the Preserver, is depicted as a god with four hands holding a lotus, mace, conch, and discus. These four objects can be compared with the four suits of the Tarot. Vishnu also has ten incarnations which correspond numerically to the ten Sepiroth of the Tree of Life and the ten pip cards in each card suit.

At the end of the fourteenth century, large groups of people were driven from India by the Islamic ruler Timur Lenk, who conquered much of central Asia. Many of the banished groups wandered to Europe bringing cards used for divination. However, cards were supposedly brought to Europe as early as the seventh century by the Arabs.

During the fifteenth century, the Tarot cards received much attention and use in Italy. By the sixteenth century, the cards gained popularity and had spread to France. The French occult revival in the nineteenth century caused the Tarot's popularity to soar.

The Torah is the Hebrew system of organizing all knowledge and experience. Many scholars believe the Tarot is the development or offspring of the Torah or Hebrew alphabet since the two relate in theme and number.

Hebrew letter	Meaning	Tarot Correspondent
Aleph	Bull, ox	The Fool
Beth	House	Magician
Gimel	Camel	High Priestess
Daleth	Womb	Empress
Heh	Window	Emperor
Vav	Nail, hook	Hierophant
Zain	Sword, weapon	Lovers
Cheth	Fence	Chariot
Veth	Snake	Strength
Yod	Open hand	Hermit
Kapth	Closed hand	Wheel of Fortune
Lamed	Ox goad	Justice
Mem	Water	Hanged Man
Nun	Fish	Death
Samekh	Tent peg	Temperance
Ayin	Eye	Devil
Peh	Mouth	Tower
Tzaddi	Fish hook	Star
Qoph	Head	Moon
Resh	Head and face	Sun
Shin	Tooth	Judgment
Tav	Mark	World

Another theory suggests the Tarot originated in Morocco. Fez became the intellectual center of the world after the ruin of Alexandria. Sages gathered there from all corners of the world but had a difficult time communicating since they spoke different languages.

To overcome the language barrier, a group of them invented a series of pictures and symbols: the Tarot. This method was used to contain their combined wisdom in a way that could be understood universally. The messages could be interpreted by anyone who learned how to decipher the allegorical messages.

All of the above are interesting theories on the Tarot' s origin, but the mystery is still unsolved. One thing is certain; whoever the creator(s) of the Tarot, they were truly ingenious and have left a most provocative phenomenon for mankind to contemplate and from which to learn.

Structure

The Tarot was designed with psychic images to be used as tools to realize the higher, inner self. The cards contain wisdom that is ageless and, being allegorical, universal. The cards are divided into two main parts, the Major Arcana and the Minor Arcana.

The Major Arcana is actually a complete Tarot deck in itself. The twenty-two cards, viewed in numerical sequence, show the internal stages of the development of consciousness. It starts at the most basic and undeveloped level represented by the Fool (0), and leads to the most complex level and ultimate goal of liberation, the World (21).

Each card in the Major Arcana contains its concentrated individual concept. Yet also, each card relates together in a calculated order to reveal the secrets of the body, soul, and spirit operating in harmony with the elemental and spiritual forces of the universe.

The Major Arcana is divided into three groups of seven, or septenaries. Distinct from the three groups is the Fool.

The Fool is the unnumbered or zero card. Given the number zero, the Fool may appear to be a card of less importance than the others since zero signifies nothing. However, zero is of such importance that the system of measurement could not exist without it. Neither could the Tarot exist without the Fool.

The Fool symbolizes a state of nothingness or lack of form from which all things emanate. He represents the dynamic force of energy in motion that causes the impulse to act or to take the first step. He is the energy behind the action.

The Fool's position in the Tarot is infinite. The Fool relates to and unites all the cards. The author has placed it at the beginning to symbolize the cyclic whirling forces of energy before the first manifestation. It also can be placed after the World (21). Not counting the Fool, the World is the last card in this sphere of existence and the first in the next sphere, which is heaven.

The first septenary of the Major Arcana includes: the Magician, the High Priestess, the Empress, the Emperor, the Hierophant, the Lovers, and the Chariot. Basically, these seven cards are the collective traits or qualities personified. They represent the forces of the dynamic psyche.

The second septenary of the Major Arcana contains the cards numbered from eight to fourteen. They are: Strength, the Hermit, the Wheel of Fortune, Justice, the Hanged Man, Death, and Temperance. This group makes clear the Spiritual influence, the position of the soul affected by the ways and variable laws of the universe and cause and effect.

The third septenary includes the cards numbered from fifteen to twenty-one. They are: the Devil, the Tower, the Star, the Moon, the Sun, Judgment, and the World. This third group pertains to the higher, complex, yet more basic and pure forces of existence.

The Major Arcana can be used without the Minor Arcana for divination. It is the part of the deck used for meditation. Both divination and meditation will be discussed in a later chapter.

The Minor Arcana is divided into four suits: Rods, Cups, Swords, and Pentacles. The four suits represent the Divine Forces in action on each sphere and level of nature. Each suit contains four court cards and ten pip cards from ace to ten.

The court cards in the Tarot deck contain four royalty cards as opposed to the three court cards in the modern playing card deck. The court cards include a king, queen, knight, and page.

The King represents the Spirit; the archetypal man. He is the personification of the governing principle characteristic of his suit. In readings he is apt to represent an older established man or firm.

The Queen represents the Soul; the archetypal women. She is a mature woman personifying the female influence characteristic of her suit.

The Knight symbolizes the Ego. He is a young person out in the world, or moving forces in a situation related to his suit. He represents the development of the soul.

The Page represents the body; a being not yet fully developed or out in the world.

The numbered cards of the Tarot develop from the Ace, which is the essence of the suit's meaning, to ten. The four objects used to represent the suits are pictured in the amount of the number of each card. For example, the Four of Rods contains four rods.

Kabalah and the Suits

The Hermetic Order of the Golden Dawn was founded in London, England during the late nineteenth century by A.F.A. Woodford, Dr. Woodman, and Dr. W. Wescott. Their purpose was to unite all occult knowledge into one ring of esoteric thought. The Golden Dawn conjoined the Tarot to the Kabalah, an ancient occult theosophy based upon esoteric meanings of the Hebrew Scriptures. The wisdom of the Kabalah is hidden behind a system of numbers and letters. The main concept is ``That Which Is, That Which Shall Be'' symbolized by the Roman numerals, IHVH. This concept is broken down into four worlds which correspond to the four suits of the Tarot. They are listed below along with a description of the characteristic of each suit.

I   The Archetypal World of pure ideas is represented by the Suit of Rods, sometimes referred to as Wands. Rods symbolize primal energy, will, and growth. They also represent agriculture, nature, inspiration, determination, strength, force, and intelligence. The Rod's element is fire.

H   The Creative World and the ability to put an idea into a pattern are represented by the Suit of Cups. Cups represent love, emotions, feelings, sensitivity, and family life. The element assigned to Cups is water, which is the symbol of the unconscious imagination, creativity, and deep thought.

V   The Formative World of expression is represented by the Suit of Swords. The Sword's element is air, gases, and the life energy. Characteristics of this suit are action, change, force, movement; sometimes war, trouble, and strife. Included are people in the military, politics, and people who are forceful and aggressive with analytical minds.

H   The Material World of visible physical objects is represented by the Suit of Pentacles. Their element is earth and its solidity. Pentacles represent industry, business, commerce, trade, and financial awards. They also represent the comfort and security that come with financial success.

The Kabalist philosophy is illustrated in the Tree of Life, a system of arranging the various levels of consciousness. In the diagram of the Tree of Life are the names of each Sepiroth (stage) and their translated meanings. Ain Soph Aour is the Godhead or Life Source. Malkuth represents earth and man's physical body. The theme of the numbered cards of the Lesser Arcana relate to the theme of the same number Sepiroth. The twenty-two cards of the Major Arcana which describe physical and spiritual forces constantly in operation relate to the twenty-two connecting paths of the Tree of Life.

The Tarot, used as a tool for meditation of the ascending spheres of the Tree of Life, enables one to understand and deal with that level, thus heightening consciousness.

TREE OF LIFE

Kether:	Crown	Tiphareth:	Beauty
Chokmah:	Wisdom	Netzach:	Victory
Binah:	Understanding	Hod:	Splendor
Chesed:	Mercy	Yesod:	Foundation
Geburah:	Severity	Malkuth:	Kingdom

AIN SOPH AOUR

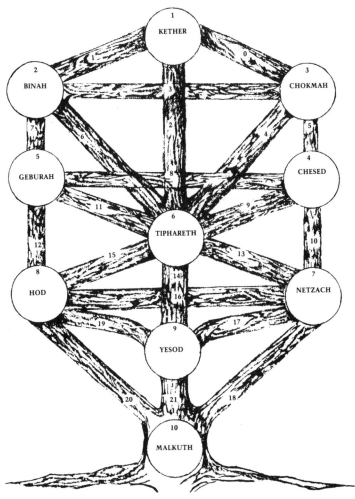

The twenty-two numbered segments are the twenty-two connecting paths that have been related to the Tarot.

Numerology and the Tarot

Numerology is the occult meaning of numbers concerning their influence on life. The Tarot cards incorporate numerology to express itself since the meaning of numbers is ageless, changeless, and has the same connotation universally.

In the Minor Arcana, an essential part of the meaning of a card is derived from the knowledge of its number in relation to its suit. Numerology is also incorporated into the Major Arcana.

NUMEROLOGY

Zero—Infinite nothingness, boundless, limitless, pure energy, bliss, superconsciousness, beyond beginning.

One—Alpha. The first, the start, the seed, the beginning. Creation from dust. Nonmanifest to manifest. Singularity. Individuality. Oneness of human. I am. Positive action.

Two—Adding on another force. Knowledge. Opposites. Mental and physical, masculine and feminine. Positive and negative. Balancing opposite forces. Action. Reasoning. Wisdom. Duality.

Three—Object of creation. Childbirth. Multiplication. Development of the seed (ONE) in union with the earth (TWO) produces a plant (THREE). The product resulting from the creation. Growth. Visible material result of ideas and action. Harmony.

Four—Memory. Logical mental reasoning by the physical man full of Spirit. Being able to express oneself in a socially accepted way in the material universe. Measurement. The reality of life on earth and being able to express oneself in it.

Five—Changing. Lack of stability. Uncontrollable force. Adversity. Wondering where you belong in society, in the world. Unhappy. Destructive energy. Moral law. Creative thought.

Six—Success. Equilibrium. Self acceptance in chosen field of life work or duty. Enthusiasm. Hope. Love. Harmony. Satisfaction. Beauty. Cooperation.

Seven—Soul Development. Safety. Security. Evaluation. Perfection. Successful completion of goals, but effort must continue. Mystery. Fate. Intuition. Number of Occult Intelligence.

Eight—Rhythm and Balance. Justice, ability to judge. Peace. Understanding. Strength. Open-mindedness. Perfect intelligence. Health. Wealth. Regeneration. Opposite force. Discarding old ideas for new. Infinity.

Nine—Attainment of a goal. Fulfillment. Completion of a cycle. Foundation to begin with new cycle. Phase before moving on to a much higher level of understanding.

Ten—Completed force, be it positive or negative. Perfection. Understanding.

To determine personal numeral influence, add all the numbers in your birthdate. For example: 3/20/57 would equal $3 + 2 + 0 + 5 + 7 = 17$, and $1 + 7 = 8$.

The Major Arcana

KEY 0

THE FOOL

Astrological Influence: The planet Uranus symbolizes that which has potential to be constructive or destructive.

Numeral Influence: Before beginning (0).

A youth is seen taking the first step to begin a journey into the future. He appears to be stepping off a cliff, quite unaware of the imminent danger. Rather, his attention is fixed expectantly ahead.

Over his shoulder is a rod which contains, in the handkerchief tied to it, knowledge gained in a previous existence. The knowledge will aid him in overcoming obstacles that will inevitably arise during his journey. The rod in his left hand is used as a walking stick. The rod symbolizes the spiritual unity and nature of all things. The white rose which he also holds in this hand represents purity and innocence.

The Fool wears a red plume, which indicates faith, on a leafy wreath around his head. The wreath indicates his connection with nature. The multicolored garments of white, red, green, and black refer to the elements and influences to which the Fool is exposed. The multiple colors also confirms his seemingly irrational, choose-at-random attitude.

A small white dog jumps and bites his left sleeve, but the Fool seems totally unaware. He is activated by impulse and the subconscious mind rather than reason. Although there is no one about to help him as he takes the step leading off the cliff, the warm sun shining upon him indicates spiritual guidance and blessing.

The Fool is potential that is not yet applied to anything. He is the manifestation of energy from within; the human personality not yet in motion. He symbolizes one who is on the outside of systemized, orderly living while adapting to a new life. He is eager to experience and develop himself and nature to its fullest potential.

The Fool is the manifestation of a new cycle of existence. He is starting anew, and since he is unaware of what direction in which to proceed, he acts upon impulse. He has the choice of many different roads and is open-minded to all of them. Not being a discriminating sort, he is open to endless possibilities, new ideas and experiences.

Key 0 indicates the space before the start of a new cycle that will require decisions and action. The period is a carefree one without pressure, but also without direction.

Divinatory Meaning: Space before a decision or choice is made. A new cycle is about to begin that the seeker will enter inexperienced. New and endless possibilities.

Reversed: Lack of effort. Immaturity. An irresponsible personality. Fear of advancing. Reckless abandonment of the senses.

KEY 1

THE MAGICIAN

Astrological Influence: Mercury, the planet closest to the sun, rules the intellect. Mercury was the legendary magician and transformer.

Numeral Influence: Singularity, or the oneness of the human personality, is represented by one.

The Magician's right hand directs a wand toward the heavens from which he receives his power. The wand symbolizes direction, intensity, and purification. His left hand points to earth where he manifests the power attained from above.

Through his powerful will, the Magician has gained control over the elements represented on the round table before him. They are the Tarot symbols of Cup (water), Rod (fire), Sword (air), and Pentacle (earth). The cup is full and bears green leaves. The Magician is working within the confines of a sturdy wall. Trees and plants flourish around him within the walls. The red rose to his left represents that which has been cultivated to grow to its most perfect state. The lilies to his left represent purity of motivation.

Above the Magician's head is a horizontal eight, the cosmic lemniscate, symbol of eternal life and dominion; the harmonious universe. Wrapped around his waist is a snake who devours its own tail, symbolizing eternity. He wears a white robe which indicates pure ideas and motives. It is covered by a red hooded cape, which symbolizes desire and discretion, which is clasped at the neck by a smaller version of the lemniscate. The gold band around the Magician's head is the Egyptian symbol of the divine spark in man, put forth by God.

The Magician's intense desire for knowledge and tremendous ability of concentration are furthered by his strong will. The control he has over the mind is evident in his actions and creations. He uses the five senses to their fullest capacity and has developed a sixth sense. Through his personal will, he is a transmitter of the Divine Will put to work on the physical plane.

Divinatory Meaning: Will and determination to see an idea or project through. Skill to organize and direct. Concentration and control. Desires fulfilled by a strong will and the ability to utilize one's innate faculties to their fullest advantage. Originality and invention.

Reversed: Abuse of power. Lack of concentration and determination to see a project through. Trickery; deceit.

KEY 2

THE HIGH PRIESTESS

Astrological Influence: The moon is the astrological symbol of the personality and subconscious. The moon's pale light creates mystery and illusion when the shadows it casts keep things hidden from view.

Numeral Influence: The meeting of opposites and the addition of another force is represented by the number two.

The High Priestess is the personification of the female. She is seated on a cube symbolic of earth between two pillars of the mystic temple. The pillar on the left, Boaz, is black and represents the negative life force. The pillar on the right, Jachin, is white and represents the positive life force. A veil is draped across the two pillars preventing the view of the internal world of the psyche and of existence. The veil is purple with a magenta lining. To the lower left and right, water can be seen, but the rest of the sanctuary is well concealed by the veil.

The High Priestess wears flowing robes of blue, the color associated with the moon and water. A thick silver band, which is considered the metal of the moon, is on her left wrist. The solar cross on her chest indicates the union of the positive and negative. The scroll on her lap is the Torah, the Hebrew Law, which contains the secret knowledge of nature and the universe.

Her feet rest upon a crescent moon, which represents the cyclic phases and reflects Divine Light. The crescent moon signifies meditation, reflection on heaven, infinity. On the crown is a smaller lunar crescent which suggests imagination and instinctive contact with higher beings. The High Priestess is an aspect of Isis, goddess of the night.

The High Priestess attracts and beckons one to discover and learn the secrets the veil keeps hidden. Her wisdom must be acquired, however, before proceeding to pass beyond the boundary she guards.

The High Priestess represents intuition and the subconscious mind which is the basis of conscious thought and action. Her female state is capable of reproduction but has not realized the male life force.

Key 2 is the stage of gaining wisdom and knowledge. It is the stage where the opposites of masculine and feminine, mental and physical, positive and negative, are balanced. Ideas and potential are realized but not yet developed or expressed.

Divinatory Meaning: Knowledge, education, wisdom. Creative ability. Secrets. Undeveloped talents. Feminine influence. Perception, self-motivation, effort. Mystery. Interest in the unknown.

Reversed: Egotism. Vanity. Immorality. Superficiality.

III — THE EMPRESS

KEY 3

THE EMPRESS

Astrological Influence: Venus is the planet which represents love, harmony, and productivity.

Numeral Influence: Three represents the object of creation.

The Empress sits comfortably in a fertile landscape of trees and plants. She appears to be pregnant, wearing an elaborate yellow and green flowing robe. Her pregnancy is an expression of the sexual union between male and female.

The waterfall that splashes into a deep pool in the background signifies the subconscious and psychic activity. Wheat, which represents the brief life span, is ready for harvest by her right. She holds six strands of wheat in her left hand with a sacred lotus flower in full bloom. The lotus flower represents the macrocosm and its center symbolizes the Life-Force or Divine One.

In her right hand the Empress holds a gold shield bearing the emblem of a red eagle. The eagle signifies immortality, prayer, the daylight, and grandeur. It also signifies the male aspect of procreation. The emblem of an eagle on the shield refers to the resplendent soul enfolded in spirituality.

On her chest is a red heart symbolic of her warmth and love. The heart is the center of harmony between the mind and sex organs. It is topped by a holy cross which represents the Spirit on a Higher Plane (+).

A crescent moon which represents a reflective, meditative nature and natural contact with higher forces, is under her left foot. A pomegranate, symbol of the unity of the complex forces of the universe, rests by her foot in front of the crescent moon. The pomegranate, being a fruit with many seeds, also symbolizes fertility and reproduction.

Mother Nature is personified by the Empress. Her fertile presence means a healthy and productive crop in agriculture. Comfort and abundance are the results of her conscientious labor.

The Empress expresses the powers that were present, but not in use, by the High Priestess. She nurtures what is hers and is instinctively protective. A deductive reasoner, the Empress manages her affairs in an orderly conservative manner.

Divinatory Meaning: Fertility, creativity, and imagination. Pregnancy. The ability to create a warm and productive environment. Good harvest. Comfort and excess. Material gain, luxurious surroundings. Productivity. Protectiveness.

Reversed Meaning: Poor mental or physical health. Unproductive. Wasteful. Dissipation of funds. Unstable. Trouble with pregnancy. Poverty.

IV — THE EMPEROR

KEY 4

THE EMPEROR

Astrological Influence: Aries, the Ram, governs the head and the ability to reason. Aries represents leadership and is an energetic and forceful sign.

Numeral Influence: Logical, stable reasoning and measurement. (4).

The Emperor sits with assurance on his throne which is decorated on its arms with the Aries' ram head. He holds the scepter of male potency in his right hand. The scepter is topped by an orb of the world surmounted by a solar cross. In his left hand is the sword with which he governs, pointed toward the earth. Tall rigid mountains of rocks are in the background. A river winds its way along the face of the mountains. The Emperor's throne is red, the color of fire and intense, invigorating activity. A strong eagle with a mighty presence supports the side of his throne. The eagle is the symbol of infinite space and the superior forces of nature. Eagles also represent the thunderbolt and fire and the father. They also symbolize male potency. Crowns represent the highest faculty in the human. The Emperor's crown is decorated by the head of an eagle with an alert expression. His clothes are the colors of the earth which he rules. Although his legs are crossed, he leans forward in readiness. He wears thick golden bracelets, the metal of the sun.

The Emperor is a respected man of authority and leadership. He bases his decisions upon external facts and does not delve beneath the surface to understand the cause and effect. He can be insensitive and overbearing and stands fast by his decisions.

Psychologically, the Emperor expresses the ability to communicate in a socially accepted way in the material universe. The Emperor is an organized man who symbolizes the male force and paternity. He represents the mate of the Empress.

Divinatory Meaning: Leadership, dominance, authority. Government in control. Discipline. Reasoning.

KEY 5

THE HIEROPHANT

Astrological Influence: Taurus, the bull, is stubborn and set in his ways.

Numeral Influence: Moral law in society (5).

A man dressed in the traditional attire of the pope sits regally before two pillars. His right hand is lifted towards the heavens, with two fingers raised and two fingers pointing down to form the sign of benediction. A lunar crescent fastens the neck of the red cape which is worn over a yellow-hued gown. His hands are gloved.

The Hierophant, which the card is named, is actually the title of the High Priest who was the head of the mysteries of Demeter. The celebration was held at the Goddess temple in Eleusis, near Athens. The Hierophant presided over the Eleusinian mysteries which were rites that took place in the temple at night. Neophytes were subjected to diverse tests in order to be initiated into the mysteries. They were under threat of punishment if they revealed any of the secrets made known to them during the ceremonies.

The crossed keys at the bottom of the card are the keys of the conscious and subconscious mind. The keys unlock the gates of heaven and hell. The silver key represents the moon and the subconscious. The gold key represents the sun and the conscious.

The Hierophant is the personification of the rules and guidelines of the spiritual life. He enforces tradition and ritual. Key 5 also represents theology.

Divinatory Meaning: Religious influence. Conformity. An inspirational teacher who reveals signs of spiritual importance. Gateways to higher consciousness reached in a ritualized manner.

Reversed: The unconventional personality. Nonconformer. Indecision and carelessness.

KEY 6

THE LOVERS

Astrological Influence: Gemini, the twins, represents duality, stimulation, and choice.

Numeral Influence: Love, enthusiasm, and self-acceptance (6).

A man and a woman embrace in their natural state in a garden of pure white lilies. Five white lilies are in full bloom around them. The wavy green leaves that grow abundantly around the Lovers represent wisdom and nature growing to its fullest expressions. The couple's arms are wrapped around each other in a mood of pure love, passion, and desire. They exchange mirrored looks of understanding and trust. Their hair flows freely as does their affection and joy. A warm golden aura glows above them.

The Lovers symbolize the harmonizing of polar opposites, that is, male and female. Through their union comes the spiritual expression of infinite oneness.

Both of the Lovers' hair is long and free-flowing. Symbolically, hair that grows from the top of the head is connected with the energetic or higher spiritual forces. That it is free-flowing indicates the instinctive, active powers of the cosmos. The man's hair is brown, symbolic of earthly energy. The woman's hair is copper, referring to the attributes of Venus, the goddess of love.

The Lovers indicate an archetypal Adam and Eve, pure and innocent. They also represent a complete, affectionate, sexual, and all-accepting love between a woman and a man.

Key 6 presents the stage where the individual personality makes its first choice or decision. The subconscious forms its own identity by desiring something outside that which it has been previously taught or shown. It is a time of choice, of decisions made independently, without overt parental or social influence, although there can be parental and external interference.

The Lovers must accept and exercise their power of choice in order to recognize their individuality apart from previous influences. Choosing a lover, in effect, is stating one's independence and personal control over one's own thoughts and actions.

Divinatory Meaning: True love and equality between a man and a woman. Temptation, choice, and decision. The personality takes control over its own choices, actions, and direction. Decisions based upon intuition rather than intellect.

Reversed: Parental or external interference has a negative effect upon a love affair or marriage. Infidelity. Vice.

KEY 7

THE CHARIOT

Astrological Influence: Cancer, the crab, is the receptive, watery sign. Cancer represents that which protects its soft interior by a hard shell or exterior.

Numeral Influence: Soul development, evaluation, and security (7).

A fair-haired charioteer holds firmly to the reins of two horses, trying to keep his vehicle on the correct path. Upon his head is a crown decorated by three pentagrams. The crown represents the highest attainment of man in the spiritual evolution. The three pentagrams on the crown refer to the higher nature of man and psychic equilibrium.

The charioteer's cape is clasped at the shoulders by two lunar crescents which face upwards and outwards. They indicate meditation inspired by and reflective of the Divine Light. Outward facing crescents also refer to the formative world.

The emblem of Cancer on the charioteer's belt suggests he is receptive to universal forces which could intervene and deter him from the Spiritual Path. Being receptive to such forces, the charioteer must apply strong will and restraint in order to keep his vehicle on the right path for spiritual progress. The scepter, a symbol of authority and triumph, indicates he will succeed.

A veil of psychic protection covers the chariot. The wheels represent the energy of circular motion in the cosmos.

The horses pulling the chariot are black and white. Horses are symbolic of the Life-force and the cosmos. Their opposite colors represent the opposing forces of positive and negative, good and evil, material and spiritual, which tug at the soul and must be kept in responsible control. The thick wooden yoke harnesses the two horses together while they both struggle to run in different directions.

The Chariot symbolizes the personality which carries one through life. Chariots have long been the symbol of both celestial bodies and of the human journey on earth. They also represent the human body's transitory nature as it is affected by mundane life forces.

The charioteer utilizes all forces to insure steady and progressive travel along the One Path. His singleness of purpose and concentrated effort to achieve his goal insure success.

The Chariot completes the first septenary of the Major Arcana. Thus, it represents the perfected and controlled state of the personality, the Higher Principles of human nature.

Divinatory Meaning: Protecting one's interest and psyche. Control of the direction of one's life. Travel. Understanding the nature of good and evil.

Reversed Meaning: Lack of control. Lack of vision causes one to stumble along without direction.

KEY 8

STRENGTH

Astrological Influence: Leo, the lion, represents strength, self-righteousness and dominance over negative forces.

Numeral Influence: Strength, health, rhythm, and balance (8).

Strength is personified by a woman who holds the mouth of a lion. She demonstrates the control of higher nature over animal forces. The white flowing gown she wears suggests purity of motivation. The wreath of wild flowers around her head represents the fullest, most beautiful expression of nature and transient life. Palm trees that grow in the background indicate fecundity and victory. Carl Jung associated the palm tree with the anima. Steep mountains represent elevated intellect.

The woman in Key 8 represents the innate female perception and motivation to create orderly progress. She is able to contemplate all planes and forces of existence. She naturally wards off and is liberated from negative interference.

The lion, considered the king and the most powerful male of the animal kingdom, is completely under the woman's control. She calmly holds his jaw with her left hand and the top of his nose with her right hand. This prevents the lion's natural inclination to attack. The woman's left arm (side of the subconscious) indicates mental effort, and the right arm (side of the conscious) indicates physical effort.

The combined forces of the woman's mental and physical effort have subdued the lion's fierce nature and have kept his basic instincts under control.

By accurately judging the internal and external nature of the lion, the woman is able to stabilize him and make him useful. Thus, she raises his level of productivity and usefulness.

All living things have a useful and higher nature that can be brought out by one in perfect balance of mental and physical capacities. Physical health is necessary for mental health.

Vitamin deficiency affects the psyche by causing disorder and unclear thinking, which lead to poor physical performance. Healthy diet and exercise are mandatory for total strength.

Divinatory Meaning: Mental and physical strength and health. The ability to cultivate latent potential to a higher, more developed state. A well-balanced body and mind.

Reversed: Letting the aspects of the lower self take control. Weakness and fear. Ill health. Vapid.

KEY 9

THE HERMIT

Astrological Influence: Virgo, the symbol of perfection and the realization of goals.

Numeral Influence: The completion of a cycle which will be the foundation to begin a new cycle. Attainment and fulfillment (9).

The Hermit stands alone on a snow-covered mountaintop with all his possessions: a cloak, walking stick, and a lantern which he holds high to light the way for others.

The Hermit's cloak is brown, a color which refers to humbleness. Cloaks symbolize alienation and withdrawal from society and the world. They also symbolize an advanced state of mind. The hood refers to personal thoughts that are unknown to others. The walking stick which he holds in his left hand is taller than the Hermit. His hair and beard are white, symbolic of the wisdom of the ages. Inside the lantern burns the Light of Perfect Knowledge from intuition. The light illuminates a small area, then reveals a larger area. The hermit represents one who is intent on perfecting his soul and developing his awareness to attain a higher level of consciousness than that which he has. He has abandoned the material comforts and security of people which at one time seemed so necessary to him. He seeks in solitude the something higher he knows exists, a solitude which is necessary to allow his own thoughts to influence him, not society's. Alone, the hermit may delve deeper into his own mind's source because he knows therein lies the answer. Research by

Carl Jung concludes that, when one has been alone for an extended period of time, one's psyche produces visions and revelations. The hermit's quest is to find the truth of his soul's existence in the revelations of his psyche.

So far advanced and incomprehensible is the Hermit's wisdom to most that he finds it difficult to relate to any but those few fellow seekers who have gone the same road. However, he is willing to help light the way for others if they care to listen.

Divinatory Meaning: A time for soul-searching. The need to step back and reevaluate goals. Search for something more than what you have. Listen to advice from wise soul. Keep an open mind to new concepts. Meditation.

Reversed: Closed mind. Locked into a stubborn way of looking at things, therefore no chance for personal growth. Refusal to listen or see through the surface of things. Isolation.

KEY 10

THE WHEEL OF FORTUNE

Astrological Influence: Jupiter governs circular motion and is considered to be the comprehensive, reasoning planet.

Numeral Influence: Individual personality (1) with limitless energy (0).

The Hand of Fate comes forth from a billowing cloud to spin the Wheel of Fortune. The cloud refers to the Universal Mind. The hand refers to a higher force and the determining cause by which things happen. The wheel signifies rotation, movement, revolution, and the cycles of existence.

A King and Queen enjoy the highest point in the cyclic phase of existence. They are on top of the wheel and their crowns indicate their eminent position. The King looks to the past, happily reviewing his rise to the top. He holds the Queen's hand in one hand, and a cup signifying abundance and enjoyment of the present in the other.

The Queen is dressed in a flowing purple gown and golden crown. She seems more aware of the inevitable decline than the King. Her back is turned to the present and her head leans more towards the future than the past. She holds her gown with her right hand as it is tugged by the foot of the man who has just fallen off the wheel. This gesture is symbolic of her awareness of the transitory nature of positions and situations.

The Man who has just fallen off the wheel is a victim of the cyclical nature of existence, as are all beings.

The Wheel is a symbol of the cause and effect of the continual rhythms of the cosmos. The constant rotation of the wheel symbolizes in itself that nothing in nature is constant. It is necessary to accept the ever changing environment the wheel presents and adapt to it. What will happen most likely depends on the sum of events leading up to the present. By past thoughts, actions, and events the person can detect a pattern and probable events can be determined.

Divinatory Meaning: Fate, chance, and destiny. Cause and effect. Karma. The future depends upon that which has been done before. The laws of nature and probability. The continuation of an ongoing pattern.

Reversed: Bad luck or fate. A cycle of good or bad luck is about to change. The seeker steps outside of circulation.

KEY 11

JUSTICE

Astrological Influence: Libra, the scales of balance, represent justice, order, balance, and harmony.

Numeral Influence: Positive action (1) by the individual (1).

Justice is personified by a woman who is seated upon a massive gold throne draped with a purple veil. In her right hand is the double-edged sword which cuts through both sides of any situation so that it can be viewed clearly. The sword symbolizes psychic decisiveness and the Divine Law of the universe. It represents the Word of God; that which is true and just.

In the woman's left hand are the Scales of Balance and Equilibrium which are tipped to the right. This unbalance suggests the unfairness of earthly life. The right side symbolizes the conscious thought and the physical environment and appearance of things. This suggests that many situations are judged by what they appear to be rather than what they truly are.

Upon her head is a crown with three turrets and a jewel of square design. Squares indicate exact measurement, the ideal base or foundation. The green cape is held together by a yellow square emblem with a red circle. The square represents the severity of the Law protecting and keeping perfect the circle of heaven, eternity, and the state of oneness within. This is the arcanum of Spiritual Justice.

Justice represents the true and fair nature of things on a spiritual and physical plane. It represents the balanced, clear, and logical interpretations by the subconscious which result in fair and just actions. The well-balanced mind is surrounded by the well-balanced environment, a result of one's own doing.

Divinatory Meaning: A fair and just outcome of a matter. Good instinct and perception. A positive end to a lawsuit. Setting a confused life to order successfully. Spiritual Justice.

Reversed: Unfair judgment. Poor choices and decisions.

KEY 12

THE HANGED MAN

Astrological Influence: Neptune rules the sea.

Numeral Influence: The beginning (1) and the reasoning force (2) result in a third product of rebirth.

A man is suspended upside down, tied by his right foot to a pole balanced across two leafless, branchless trees. This pole is resting horizontally across two vertical trees which indicates ultimate change of direction. His left foot falls behind him, forming a cross. Spiritual triangles are formed by the spaces between his legs, arms, and upper body.

The Hanged Man's red pants indicate human passion and the physical state. The coat is blue, the color of infinity, with a red collar. The coat is crossed at the waist by a red belt with a gold buckle. Yellow shoes are symbolic of his high ideals. Blue tinted clouds rise gently behind him under a purple sky. The Hanged Man wears an entranced, distant expression on his still features.

Being bound to the tree indicates dependency to the physical earth including the laws of society. However, the Hanged Man's upside-down position indicates he has made a complete reversal in his dependency. Coins can fall from his pockets symbolizing the rejection of materialistic values.

The Hanged Man has been awakened spiritually and, with renewed awareness, he will work faithfully to develop his consciousness toward the Universal Mind. He has overcome forces and now freely submits himself to God, the great force of Universal Law.

The Hanged Man will be living in opposite fashion to most people, but will not flaunt it. Instead, he will pursue his goal silently and in harmony with himself and the universe. The inner peace he has attained will be reflected in his dealing with other people.

Divinatory Meaning: Spiritual awareness and the happiness and assuredness it brings. Sacrificing for a noble purpose. Reversal of one's current way of life. Inner peace. Developed intuition and prophecy.

Reversed: A selfish, materialistic personality. Failure to find the true meaning of one's existence. Concern only with physical matters. Spiritual emptiness.

KEY 13

DEATH

Astrological Influence: Scorpio governs the reproductive organs. Scorpio is also related to the eighth house of the Zodiac, the house of death.

Numeral Influence: The beginning (1) and the product (3) combined equal four. Four represents organization and the reality of life on earth which inevitably leads to physical death.

Death is personified as an eerie white skeleton draped in a black robe. The skeleton itself represents that which survives death. The skull represents human immortality.

The mystery of Death is concealed by a large, black-hooded robe. Black indicates that which is negative. The black hood has a purple lining, which is the color of death. It is clasped at the neck by a golden square which indicates the Divine Law.

Death clears the path to the beyond with a large silver-bladed scythe. The scythe represents harvest, hope, and rebirth. The white rose represents the beauty, immortality, and freedom of the soul.

A bird, which indicates the human soul, flies toward the red sun of immortality. A winding river which reflects the sun's red glow is symbolic of nature's phenomena of creation, growth, death, and rebirth.

Death represents the inevitable transformation of all living things. It terminates the outworn and unproductive and thus liberates them. Death represents a metamorphic change.

Key 13 does not represent physical death as much as it represents death of a phase of life or characteristic that is outworn. The purpose of this arcanum is to show the concept of death as a means to the renewal of life.

Death of the old self had to occur for the Hanged Man because a complete change was necessary for the advancement of his consciousness. After the death of the old self comes the rebirth; the renewal. The Hanged Man did not physically die; his old way of thinking did.

The immortality and the freedom of the soul is released from the transformed being in Key 13.

Divinatory Meaning: The end of a particular phase, epoch, or feeling. The present situation is outworn, unproductive, so it will end soon. A major change is due. Termination of an unendurable situation. Renewal.

Reversed: Catastrophe, disorder, and panic.

KEY 14

TEMPERANCE

Astrological Influence: Sagittarius governs the hips and thighs which support the body. Sagittarius is the restless intellect symbolized by the Archer.

Numeral Influence: Beginning (1) of organization and logical mental reasoning by the physical human who is full of Spirit (4).

The hermaphroditic figure of an archangel, clothed in a pure white robe, pours the waters of life between two gold cups. The water flow equalizes the stream between the cup of the subconscious and the cup of the superconscious. The water ripples as it flows, representing the cosmic vibration of the universe and the constant cyclic process of formation, regeneration, and purification. The transferring of water in the cups also refers to the raising of that which is low to a higher plane.

The archangel stands with one foot on the physical world and one foot submerged in the pool of the soul. The red spiritual triangle on the angel's robe refers to the Trinity. The peak of the triangle is the irradiating point to which all within the triangle are instinctively drawn.

The wings of the angel suggest motion and progress in spiritual illumination. A shining aura emanates from the spiritual psyche. A path leads from the pool to a light which glows over the mountains of wisdom and understanding in the distance. Three yellow irises and the bud of a fourth suggest radiance and promise.

Temperance is the perfect harmony of the universal psychic and material vibrations. It represents an exact mix and balance. The subconscious and the self-conscious are united in a state harmonious with the vibration of the universe.

The Temperance card refers to moderation and control. The intellect drives one to experience different ideas in trying to organize a productive existence. One must finally learn to adapt to the life from which the soul can most benefit.

Overindulgence in any one aspect or physical action in life can deter this progress. The archangel warns that excess in any state or form is a deterrent from the One Path. The archangel guides the soul to the Path of Spiritual Enlightenment.

Divinatory Meaning: Moderation and control in all actions and affairs. Adapting to new circumstances. Diplomacy. Even temperament. Harmonizing of the psychic and material aspects.

Reversed: Unstable efforts and actions. Mood swings. Emotional unbalance.

KEY 15

THE DEVIL

Astrological Influence: Capricorn, the Goat, is the governor of the knees. Capricorn tends to be a sign with materialistic values.

Numeral Influence: Beginning (1) of unhappiness and confusion (5).

The devil is portrayed by the animal head of a goat. His eyes are yellow and evil. Two twisted horns, symbolic of his power and persistence to mislead, extend from his head. An inverted pentacle, which symbolizes the infernal in Black Magic, is set between his horns. The fly, symbolic of the Devil's incessantly evil nature, is in the center of the inverted pentagram. A burning candle, which represents individual life as opposed to universal or cosmic life, suggests his power is limited to influence only the individual lives that fall into his trap.

The Devil's head is framed by a red circle which refers to physical life, passion, and aggression. The base of the card is in darkness.

The grotesque figure of the devil is the symbol of the evil that can cause one to lose one's way. He is the negative force that steers one off the road to the One Goal by tempting one with illusions and with false promise of earthly happiness. Where the angel in Key 14 guides the soul to spiritual enlightenment, the devil misleads the soul into spiritual darkness. He is the deterrent warned of in Key 14.

The Devil leads the mind into a void of psychic emptiness. Being too weak to recognize or combat the desires that the devil evokes causes one to end up not unlike the man and woman who, in another interpretation of the Devil card, lose their freedom and end up chained to the Devil. It is the vulnerability and greed in humans that leads to destruction.

By rejecting materialistic values and being able to see the real meaning behind illusions, the soul can extricate itself from the devil's grasp. Life is a continuation of trials and obstacles one must overcome while seeking the truth. Our earthly bodies are vehicles of the soul. We can either go the way of the Angel or fall by the way of the Devil.

Divinatory Meaning: Taking things for their surface value. Superficial, materialistic personality. Greed, lust, and perversion. Living in darkness. Evil influence. Lost soul. Slave to temptation and ignorance. Nothing of value will be gained.

Reversed: Rejection of materialistic values. The greedy personality realizes itself. A turn to Higher Forces for help. Rescue from a potentially damaging situation.

KEY 16

THE TOWER

Astrological Influence: The planet Mars represents human activity and force, be it constructive or destructive.

Numeral Influence: The start (1) of equilibrium, cooperation, and harmony (6).

A massive tower is struck by lightning. The vertical shape of the Tower suggests the ascent from earth to heaven. The lightning that strikes from the left and right indicates thoughts emanating from heaven to earth, with dynamic force to emphasize its meaning. Towers usually represent sturdy foundations; however, this tower was built on false values and unstable foundations.

Flames devour the inside of the tower, forcing the inhabitants to flee. A male and female figure jump from the tower, falling upside down into the crashing waves below. There is a rhythmic motion in the waves to symbolize the preservation of life; there is still hope for them. Smoky grey clouds fill the darkened sky, carrying away what once stood in tiny particles of dust.

An environment built on superficial knowledge is struck down by a momentary flash of truth and insight. From this flash of truth, the false values are realized and understood.

The material world of matter and form are transitory, but the soul is everlasting. Key 16 represents the stage where the seeker realizes this and the consequent internal change of consciousness brings external changes.

The new personality can no longer survive in old relationships or in the old environment. The unavoidable change is traumatic, but is realized to be of great value.

Divinatory Meaning: Sudden inspiration and realization. A traumatic change that will eventually bring positive growth and new awareness. A broken home. Divorce. Outgrowing the environment.

Reversed: Future growth stunted by the emotions. Lack of insight to improve stagnant matters.

KEY 17

THE STAR

Astrological Influence: Aquarius, the water carrier, is the intuitive, activist sign. Aquarians are analytical by nature and never take anything at its surface value.

Numeral Influence: Start (1) of positive action (7) to bring harmony and understanding.

A bright star radiates Divine Light above a beautiful woman. Seven lesser stars surround and reflect the great star. The female figure is nude, symbolic of the revelation of nature's mysteries. Her hair is blonde and flowing, representing spiritual contact, growth, and blessing. Her youth and beauty symbolize eternal life. The woman pours the water of psychic energy from two pitchers. The water from the blue pitcher in her right hand is poured into a pool in which her right foot is submerged. The red pitcher in her left hand is poured on the land upon which she kneels. The woman pours the water in the pool and on land to stir and reactivate life in perfect balance.

The fertile landscape indicates nature's forces behind creation. The palm tree symbolizes fecundity. A red flower is in full bloom by the woman's right knee. The red bird, symbolic of mental activity, peacefully alights on a leafy green tree in the background.

After shattering the materialistic environment in Key 16, a new life has been found. The flash of inspiration from the Spirit caused the Tower to fall and is the dominant force of this card. Inspiration from above gives the seeker insight, faith, and understanding. The conscious mind opens to accept the union of ideas and substance of the subconscious. The light of the soul inside the self is found and allowed to shine forth. The seeker's faith has been rewarded.

Divinatory Meaning: Inspiration, insight, and understanding. Mental and physical health. A new life and openness to new ideas and concepts. Guidance from above is found within. Eternal life.

Reversed: Failure to find happiness. Closed mind and narrow viewpoint. Mental and physical illness.

KEY 18

THE MOON

Astrological Influence: Pisces, the fish, is the last sign of the zodiac, and is a combination of all the characteristics of each of the twelve signs. Pisces is a psychic sign, receptive and mysterious.

Numeral Influence: Beginning (1) of perfect intelligence (8).

The waning light of the full Moon faintly illuminates the world below. The Moon affects the tides and the water in the animal body. A wolf and a dog who feel this pull howl at the mysterious light. A purple crayfish crawls up from the depths of the pool of the subconscious.

The wolf represents the wild animal kingdom. The dog represents the wolf's relative domesticated by humans. Both animals suggest the instinctive side of human nature.

The plants that line the pool of the subconscious represent the vegetable kingdom. The crayfish is the symbol of early conscious growth. The path of the seeker's journey starts from the crayfish and continues beyond the massive towers into the unknown. The two towers, one square and the other circular in shape, guard the path.

The Moon's light indicates the reflected light of the subconscious and the imagination. It casts a dim light on latent powers and potential of the seeker that were always present but had remained dormant until now. The intuition discovers the interior knowledge that the seeker needs to develop.

The Moon's light can create uncertainty and illusions because of its dimness. The seeker is warned to take care to distinguish the real from the unreal while traveling the moonlit road.

Divinatory Meaning: Psychic powers are developed. Hidden talents or feelings come to light. Situation can be illusionary. Intuition and imagination. Solitude. Peace.

Reversed: What was unclear is clear. A mystery is solved. Upset emotions.

KEY 19

THE SUN

Astrological Influence: The sun is the symbol of power and energy. It is the light of the earth.

Numeral Influence: Beginning (1) of attainment of a goal (9).

The warmth and light of the sun causes sunflowers to grow to their full capacity. Sunflowers represent the peak of nature's expression, and their many seeds suggest regeneration.

A golden-haired male and female, sometimes referred to as the Gemini twins, stand before a brick wall under the sun. Their golden hair suggests the sun's rays. The brick wall indicates division, height, and rising consciousness.

The Sun is the power of the manifest world and leads to the world beyond. Its light exposes the unclear and the mysteries kept in shadows by the moon. Perfect consciousness of the Spirit is attained. In a childlike state of love, innocence, and acceptance, the complex is simple and understood. The Sun shines upon the joyous return home.

The Sun unites all intelligence and knowledge attained by the earthly journey into one. All perfected levels of consciousness are united. The subconscious and the self-conscious blend into one. Physical limitations are liberated. The regenerated personality realizes its unity with One Will, who has ruled all from the beginning. However, although the fact that the soul is a vehicle for the Lord has been recognized, a sense of individuality still exists.

Divinatory Meaning: Happiness, pleasure, and understanding. Positive energy. Warmth, love, and growth. Joy. Accomplishment. Success.

Reversed: Unhappiness and loss. Failure in matters of importance. Simulated happiness.

KEY 20

JUDGMENT

Astrological Influence: Pluto is the underworld or dwelling place of earth-departed souls.

Numeral Influence: Adding on another force in a higher plane (2) before beginning anew (0).

A man, woman, and child awaken from the dead and reach toward the Light of the Universe. The man represents kinetic energy. The woman represents the female passive life-force of form. The child represents the union and harmony of the polarized natures of male and female. The child is the knowledge and under-standing of force and form and a symbol of regeneration. Their bodies are discolored to a blue tone to indicate they are not on this physical plane.

The trumpet that summons those to Final Liberation and Glory appears from a cloud. The trumpet awakens the soul for resurrection. Being metal, it also refers to the elements of fire and water. Red flames are blown from the clouds and trumpet. The cross symbolizes the perfect union of man and woman, God and earth.

The tomb from which they arise refers to the physical body and fleshly desires that no longer exist. The tomb floats on a golden stream of water. Bluish mountains of the intellect are seen in the background. They represent the separation of the mind from the body.

Key 20 notes the final state of personal consciousness. The sense of separateness is terminated. The everlasting soul rises to experience infinite nature; eternal life.

Divinatory Meaning: Personal consciousness blends into universal consciousness. Release. Liberation. Fulfillment. Healing.

Reversed: Fear of death is caused by misunderstanding it. Lost soul.

KEY 21

THE WORLD

Astrological Influence: Saturn symbolizes time which swallows or absorbs all its expressions into itself.

Numeral Influence: Adding on another force in a higher plane (2) to be one (1) positive force.

The female figure is free and suspended in air. A purple cloth is draped about her body. In each hand she holds a white wand which represents polarization and rotation. She represents the eternal creative activity and cyclic motion of the entire cosmos. Nature's wreath surrounds her and refers to the connection of all phases of the cosmic process. It is tied at the top by a red robe of victory. Hundreds of tiny lights sparkle within the wreath, which indicates the macrocosm in its ultimate state of restored perfection.

In the four corners of the wreath are the four figures of which John wrote in describing the throne in Revelation 4:7.

The World represents the synthesis of all separate elements, sensations, and thought. It is the Final Goal, the return of all things to the Original State. The soul is one with God. All is one. It is the perfection and unity of all things of the macrocosm in the Divine State. It is the completion of the spiritual evolution of the manifest to whence it came.

The sense of separateness and individual personality and form are done. Their work has been completed. As a complete and responsible citizen, the seeker enters the holy kingdom of heaven.

The arcanum represents the salvation from death, which is eternal life.

Divinatory Meaning: Deserved rewards. Triumph. Eternal life. Peace and joy in a new home.

Reversed: Strong attachment to an earthly place or object. Earthbound.

The Minor Arcana

The Rods

ACE OF RODS

from the clouds. The clouds are in a state of metamorphosis which makes vague the link between the spiritual and material worlds. A rod is held by the hand over fertile woodlands which represent thriving, uncontrolled vegetation. The rod is healthy and strong, bearing vibrant green leaves. Rods represent the spiritual intellect and the green leaves refer to renewal and growth.

Interpretation: The Ace of Rods is the symbol of energy, fertility, growth, and the beginning of spiritual understanding. It represents self-expression through the creation of an original idea, pattern, and product. It is a positive symbol of the soul in tune with nature and the cosmos.

Reversed: Spiritual emptiness, lack of progress, and lack of growth. Delays and cancellations.

ACE OF RODS

Description: A hand, symbolic of help from above, emerges

Interpretation: The mature strong personality is developing itself and its ideas. The necessary preparations for success in one's field of endeavor are being made. At the same time, one must make a choice to insure steady progress. Research and learning.

Reversed: Loss of interest and faith in project.

TWO OF RODS

Description: A youth firmly holds a rod bearing leaves and acorns in one hand and an orb representing the world in the other. The hand of another person (not fully in the picture) offers a second rod which is leafy although not as developed as the one the youth holds. The emblem on the shield at the youth's side is that of a crossed rose and lily. Red roses refer to desire and nature; white lilies indicate abstract thought. One rose is shaped like the mandala and the other is not yet in bloom. The hands of the youth are gloved and there is a feather in his cap. The cap refers to thought; the feather to faith.

THREE OF RODS

Description: The back of a caped figure is seen looking expectantly into the distance as though awaiting an arrival. His cape is decorated, symbolizing the solitary work and effort put into a project. He holds a leafy rod in his hand while another more developed rod is placed by his side. Behind him is a third rod bearing leaves and ripe acorns indicating developed ideas.

Interpretation: Plans are made, but help is needed to see them accomplished. Perhaps help will be offered from an established person or firm.

Reversed: Help is offered but not in one's best interest.

FOUR OF RODS

Description: Four growing rods are firmly planted in gate-like fashion in front of a castle built high on a hill. A garland of flowers decorates the four rods. Garlands symbolize that which connects or joins together in unity. White and red roses of purity and desire adorn the wreath, as well as grapes of fertility. The castle, being situated on a higher level, indicates spiritual power and watchfulness. Castles suggest that something of value is within.

Interpretation: Established home and financial life. Success is well deserved.

Reversed: Insecurity. Fortune earned must be guarded. Stay alert for continued success.

FIVE OF RODS

Description: Five rod-bearing opponents, represented by their arms only, compete against one another. Their arms are clothed differently which suggests difference of opinions and personalities. Some hands are gloved; one wrist is adorned with a heavy bracelet.

Interpretation: Competition, struggle, tension, and conflict in business or project. Disorder caused by obstacles and differing opinions.

Reversed: Trouble with contracts.

SIX OF RODS

Description: A proud man in uniform rides a well-groomed and decorated horse. He holds a rod with a red ribbon laced around it which indicates virtue. There is a laurel wreath of victory by his side. Five growing rods are planted firmly behind him.

Interpretation: Victory is gained through intelligent decisions and diplomacy. An important matter is settled successfully. Triumph after a struggle.

Reversed: Winning with no gain. False pride.

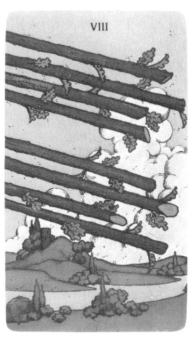

SEVEN OF RODS

Description: A bearded, mature man places a rod diagonally across six growing rods in order to guard his position. His expression is thoughtful and observant.

Interpretation: Mental and physical strength is needed to combat opposition. Constant effort and courage keeps one on top of adversaries.

Reversed: Taking on more than one can handle. Embarrassing loss.

EIGHT OF RODS

Description: Over lush green scenery and a winding river, eight rods fly through a partially clouded sky. The landscape refers to vegetation, nature, and fertility. The river refers to the creative force of nature and time.

Interpretation: Vacation; travel by air for the purpose of relaxation and enjoyment. Quick travel to a new place. Fast movement; arrival.

Reversed: Cancelled trips or engagements due to arguments.

NINE OF RODS

Description: A uniformed military man stands on guard by a group of eight rods. The ninth rod he holds over his shoulder in readiness for defense. His helmet is decorated, which indicates his constant awareness and enthusiasm to defend his position.

Interpretation: Dedication to defending one's position or situation because conflict is expected. Stable positioning and alertness insure success against attack.

Reversed: Ill health, physical injury. Failure to protect oneself adequately. Disaster.

TEN OF RODS

Description: A man in a feathered cap trudges wearily on, bowing under the burden of ten heavy rods. The cap indicates thought, and the feathers refer to the element air and to contemplation and faith.

Interpretation: Determination to see a very demanding project through to the finish. Oppression caused by too much pressure and strain.

Reversed: One must rely on oneself to alleviate one's situation.

Interpretation: A faithful youth filled with good intentions. A trustworthy person who naturally transmits spiritual information from a pure and sincere heart. Eyes covered by a hat, this youth cannot see the future, nor does he realize the enlightening revelations he conveys to others by his being.

Reversed: Illness. Bad news surrounded by rumors.

PAGE OF RODS

Description: A youth in plain clothing holds on to a thin but growing rod. His eyes are hidden by the shadow of a low, feathered hat, indicating that he cannot foresee what lies ahead. Feathers were symbolic of the creator gods in the Egyptian pantheon. Feathers are also associated with birds in flight and with faith. Mountains, which denote the ascent to a higher sphere of existence, are in the background.

KNIGHT OF RODS

Description: A knight in armor carries a rod resting on his shoulder. A ripened acorn is situated between two leaves on the rod. A salamander, impervious to fire as is his armor, decorates his glove. A dragon is perched, out of his view, on his helmet. Dragons are fiery creatures which indicate aggression and battles.

Interpretation: An energetic, restless, somewhat impulsive opportunist. Change of situation or residence. A person who is not ready to settle.

Reversed: One who succumbs to all temptations.

QUEEN OF RODS

Description: A brown-eyed, blonde-haired queen stands in the countryside holding a rod in one hand and a sunflower in the other. The sunflower represents nature in full bloom. A bud of another flower grows beneath it on the same stem. Her crown is adorned with green sprigs. Her flowing garments are in different shades of gold, the color of the sun.

Interpretation: Sincere and loyal, the charming Queen of Rods represents a nature-loving country woman fond of children and homelife. Patient and loving, she holds strong friendships and is spiritually aware.

Reversed: Jealous and unstable woman. Mistrustful and fickle.

Interpretation: A wise, intelligent, and educated man. A fatherly type, married, with family. Passionate and loyal, the King of Rods is full of ideas, and is a leader in enterprise. He prefers country living and is a conscientious sort.

Reversed: Extremely severe and critical man. Dogmatic and overbearing.

KING OF RODS

Description: The King holds a rod bearing acorns and leaves as he gazes across the countryside. He is dressed in natural earth tones and his cape is attached at the shoulder by a solar cross. Crowns indicate heightened spiritual development. Underneath the crown his head is covered, indicating contemplation and ideas.

The Cups

ACE OF CUPS

Description: A hand comes forth from a cloud offering a cup overflowing with water that streams from Paradise to the waters of earth below. A white and yellow light glows from within the cup. A white dove, symbol of spirituality in the exalted state, spreads its wing behind the cup. Pink water lilies, with eight petals signifying the intersection with the heavens and earth, grow forward to the cup.

Interpretation: The beginning of great love, joy, spiritual enlightenment, perfection, beauty. Family love and true friendships. Birth.

Reversed: Loss of love and happiness. Empty heart.

TWO OF CUPS

Description: A man and woman exchange cups in an outdoor setting. The woman wears a wreath around her head; the man, a band. They look into each other's faces with undivided attention. The wreath represents the connection between all things in nature. The golden band refers to the Divine Spark in man.

Interpretation: Mutual love and understanding shared between man and woman. Union, commitment.

Reversed: Disillusion. Conflicting interests cause partners to separate.

THREE OF CUPS

Description: Three young women, their hair adorned with wreaths of flowers, gaze ahead. Each has her own variety of flowers as well as individual eye and hair color. Before them stand three cups on a table, as well as ripe fruit. Fruit grows abundantly on vines under a blue sky.

Interpretation: Abundance, bounty, happiness, and celebration. Plenty of food, drink, and friends. Cause for celebration.

Reversed: Wanton pleasure seeker. Hedonist. Sex without love.

FOUR OF CUPS

Description: Three full cups sit nestled in ivy in the foreground. Ivy symbolizes that which is in need of help or protection. A face appears in the ivy to the left, while a hand emerges from clouds to the right offering a fourth cup. Trees grow upon a hill in the background.

Interpretation: Great opportnity offered from a helpful source. Opportunity comes when one is unaware and in a passive state of mind.

Reversed: Watch for new contacts, relationships. Resentful of help offered. Giving up or losing a great opportunity.

FIVE OF CUPS

Description: In the foreground a man stands with head bent eyeing three overturned cups, their contents spilled. Across a body of water sits a crumbling tower upon a hill. The man does not see the two cups standing upright behind him. Birds that represent human souls fly overhead.

Interpretation: Attention is fixed on misfortune and regrets. The good in life is overlooked. Disappointment and guilt. Rediscovery.

Reversed: A time for patching up misunderstandings and setting things straight.

SIX OF CUPS

Description: A boy offers a golden cup containing blossoming lilies to his female friend. In the foreground on a stone fence stand five cups filled with pure white lilies. The fence indicates the boy and girl inside are still young enough to need protection.

Interpretation: Innocent, undemanding love. Accepting one for what he or she is. Meeting with friend from the past. Nostalgia.

Reversed: Refusal to grow up or adapt to new situations. Returning to old friends or ways as a form of security when overwhelmed by difficulties.

SEVEN OF CUPS

Description: Seven cups are positioned in billowing clouds. They contain on the lowest level: an asp, which represents energy and force; a laurel wreath with a red ribbon, which represents victory; and a mask, which indicates the concealed self and what one desires to be. On the second level the two cups contain: a woman's head, which represents astral light and the spiritual life; and jewels with a butterfly resting upon them, which represents the soul. On the highest level a dragon, which indicates aggressions and combat, is in one cup, while the other cup holds a castle on a hill, which indicates the will to be saved.

Interpretation: Several choices are available, and the imagination makes them all seem grand. Focus energy on one goal to assure success.

Reversed: Determination to follow good ideas through.

EIGHT OF CUPS

Description: Eight cups are balanced in the foreground while a cloaked figure departs from them to travel into the hills. A crescent moon shines down on sparkling water. The figure has his back turned, which indicates he is leaving his present situation. The cloak represents separation. The hood refers to concealed thoughts.

Interpretation: Personal success and accomplishment that bring much satisfaction. However, disappointment in love prompts the seeker to turn and head toward something higher. Emotional dependence on friends and lover decreases. Traveling on to something new.

Reversed: One actively seeks happiness and enjoyment.

NINE OF CUPS

Description: An overweight man dressed in casual attire and a red plumed hat, wears a pleasant, satisfied expression on his face. Nine upright cups are situated on a draped table behind him, indicating abundance.

Interpretation: Self-satisfaction and contentment with friends and accomplishments. Enjoying friends, food, and drink to the hilt. Good natured and liberal personality.

Reversed: Weight gain from overeating and drinking. Others take advantage of the good-natured personality. Watch diet and drink.

TEN OF CUPS

Description: A male and female hold one cup in a pastoral spring setting. A rainbow shines from the cup, arching across the sky and extending beyond the picture. Nine cups diagonally fall across the rainbow from sky to land. The rainbow is the symbol of universal peace and harmony.

Interpretation: Contentment with the one you love, family, and friends. People who have gone through the good and bad times together feel secure and happy. Trust, much love, fine home.

Reversed: Someone unhappy in the home. Inconsideration to mate. Quarrels. A child runs away.

PAGE OF CUPS

Description: A pensive youth wears a hat draped and plumed. The large hat symbolizes meditation. Its airy plume refers to contemplation. The Page's flowing robe is decorated with red tulips. On a table in front is a cup with a fish rising above the rim suggesting the life-force surging upwards. Fish also refer to psychic ability and motion.

Interpretation: A quiet and intelligent youth. A perfectionist who is artistic, poetic, and meditative. The realization of talents.

Reversed: Frustration, bad news. A charming person but lazy and critical.

KNIGHT OF CUPS

Description: The Knight of Cups wears a suit of armor with a helmet topped with wings. Wings refer to movement and travel. His cape is clasped with the motif of a wave, which indicates forward motion. In the background is a fertile landscape including mountains and a winding river. The river refers to creativeness and time. He holds his cup before him.

Interpretation: Artistic, imaginative, poetic person who is open-minded and socially oriented. He is both convincing and easy to convince.

Reversed: One who promises rose gardens. Out of touch with reality.

QUEEN OF CUPS

Description: A fair-skinned Queen with braided hair holds a cup in front of her. Her earrings are pearl and her crown is made of sea shells. She stands before the ocean. A large fan shell is seen in the background. Shells are symbols of the ocean and of prosperous travel.

Interpretation: A kind and generous woman interested and talented in the arts. A woman who feels comfortable in any situation. An imaginative, intuitive woman characterized by expressive eyes and a gentle manner. A romantic and attractive woman touched by all she sees.

Reversed: Moody, senseless schemer. Charming troublemaker.

KING OF CUPS

Description: A fair-skinned king clothed in marine tones holds the cup of his suit and a golden scepter. A clear blue sky and deep green sea make up the background. The scepter refers to his authority. The sea is the symbol of the source of life.

Interpretation: Authoritative, responsible, ambitious man, one who demands respect. An expert in the arts, sciences, or law. A strong, powerful, and secretive man who gives excellent advice. Generous, but with a tendency to be manipulative.

Reversed: One who can bring ruin to anyone who dares cross him.

The Swords

ACE OF SWORDS

Description: A hand issues forth from a cloud holding a double-edged sword. The double-edged sword indicates justice on a higher level. A crown, from which the laurel and palm of victory and the red and white roses of desire and freedom hang, circles the sword. The crown is the symbol of prominent spiritual action and attainment. Grey mountains of intellect and reason are in the background. Clouds billow and form in the air around the sword.

Interpretation: The triumph of positive force. Victory. Freedom. The beginning of a struggle for a noble cause. Action. Power, great force, and championship.

Reversed: Pyrrhic victory, chaos. Weakness of will.

TWO OF SWORDS

Description: A woman stands blindfolded, while holding crossed swords. Blindfolded, she cannot see her situation clearly, if at all. Rocks that rise above the water's surface form small islands behind her. Rocks represent the conscious thought; water represents subconscious thought. Only a crescent of the moon is in clear view.

Interpretation: In deadlock, but a move is inevitable. Weighing consequences that are unclear and not completely understood.

Reversed: Wrong decision. Make new friends and create new situations.

THREE OF SWORDS

Description: Gloomy clouds gather over a bleeding heart. The heart symbolizes love and warmth. Here, the heart has been pierced by three swords at every angle, and the blood represents the final result of pain. The storm clouds indicate turbulent emotions and confusion.

Interpretation: Broken heart, tears, and sorrow. Emotional upheaval, pain, and disturbance. Disappointment, shattered emotions.

Reversed: Regret and depression caused by deep hurt in the past. Dwelling on old sorrows.

FOUR OF SWORDS

Description: A knight is lying down by a window, which suggests a separation from the outside world. The sky is misty and grey. One sword hovers above the knight while two others hover between him and the window. One sword is suspended outside in the mist. Autumn oak leaves and ripened acorns lay by his helmet.

Interpretation: Retreat from the outside world to rejuvenate emotional and physical strength. Reevaluation of thoughts and life in peaceful surroundings.

Reversed: Remaining in unsatisfactory surroundings. The postponement of an action or decision that must be made.

FIVE OF SWORDS

Description: A figure concealed by a dark, hooded cape gathers abandoned swords, while two dejected figures, unaware of his presence, mourn by the sea. Hooded figures indicate concealed thoughts and motives.

Interpretation: Temporary advancement. Strength and severity win a momentary triumph which, in the end, becomes humiliating.

Reversed: Unexpected turn for the worst.

Interpretation: Moving to a calmer, more peaceful place. Crossing water to arrive at a better destination. Smoothing of woes and difficulties.

Reversed: Remaining in unsatisfactory surroundings. Proposal or move postponed.

SIX OF SWORDS

Description: A man wearing warm clothing directs a boat across choppy water toward smoother waters and the land beyond. A solemn female passenger seated by his feet huddles in a cape. Six swords pierce the floor at the bow of the boat. This card can also be compared to the Night Sea Crossing, in which the sun was thought to suffer death at night (being swallowed by water) and was resurrected in the morning. This ancient expression in relation to the six of swords refers also to the woman's suffering that will lift after she crosses the night water.

SEVEN OF SWORDS

Description: A man with his face partially concealed by a furry cap runs away holding five swords that are not clearly visible in the twilight. A green sash is around his waist.

Interpretation: Theft without guilt. Greediness in taking more than is needed and mistaken confidence in so doing. Attention is given to a certain project while an old one is still in mind.

Reversed: Dwelling over past mistakes prevents progress in new projects. Pessimism. Seek advice.

EIGHT OF SWORDS

Description: A red-gowned woman's hands, legs, and face are bound. She is abandoned and feels forsaken. She cannot hear, speak, or see, but senses that her situation is temporary. Eight swords pierce the swampy area around her. Cold grey pinnacles loom in the background.

Interpretation: A temporary prisoner of the self. A withdrawn, introverted personality. Lack of confidence and motivation to make a change in one's life. Fear of failure keeps one in a rut.

Reversed: Faith in oneself is regained, wounds heal, and negative feelings fade. Slow but steady return to health and productivity.

NINE OF SWORDS

Description: Hands are seen tied at the wrist by a thick rope. Three trees are silhouetted against the red sky. Seven swords are suspended horizontally above the tied hands and two swords are suspended behind them. Ropes are symbolic of the inner path which binds the conscious mind with the substance of the spirit.

Interpretation: Productive energy is repressed and must be released. Feeling unfulfilled and useless. Bound by that which is gone and will never return. Lack of help or understanding from others.

Reversed: Movement toward productive activity.

TEN OF SWORDS

Description: A body pierced by ten swords lies helpless and bleeding in the cold snow. Blood symbolizes the final result of an epoch of extreme suffering and pain. Snow falls from a black sky, indicating a bleak and hopeless day.

Interpretation: Accepting ideas and ways of others leads to defeat and ruin. Pain and bitter disappointment; lowest point in a cycle.

Reversed: Improvement. Accept self and turn to higher forces for help.

PAGE OF SWORDS

Description: A fair-haired youth looks ahead while he gropes at his sword in feeling for a comfortable handling. Clouds form in a red sky. Three columns stand in the background; a fourth column is toppled in the dry grass. The standing columns symbolize support and stability while the fallen column indicates the opposite.

Interpretation: Youth belonging to an institution, be it military, school, or reformatory. Someone with owed time. A spy with shady character and malicious intentions.

Reversed: Safety is threatened by this person.

KNIGHT OF SWORDS

Description: A dark and dangerous looking knight stands in the reflection of flames from a burning tower. He is dressed for war and holds his sword upright, ready to meet the opposition. His elaborate helmet indicates boldness, imagination, vitality, and aggression.

Interpretation: Fearless and confident young man who is career-minded and a conqueror. He will stop at nothing and sacrifice anything to get what he wants.

Reversed: A conceited braggart interested only in himself with little or no regard for others. Extravagance.

QUEEN OF SWORDS

Description: A dark-haired woman stares penetratingly ahead with an upraised sword in her hand. Red roses bloom around her and clouds billow in the background. Red roses are symbolic of passion and desire; of beauty and cultivation. Her crown is sharp and spiked.

Interpretation: A determined, sharp-witted, and stern woman who is always on guard. She has been hurt in the past and thus retains an air of aloofness and caution. She is wise, intelligent, and intent on having her own way. She is always on guard.

Reversed: Spiteful and malicious person. Gossips with intent to malign.

KING OF SWORDS

Description: An intelligent, serious-looking King stands tall, firmly holding a double-edged sword and three strands of wheat. The double-edged sword represents true justice whose power emanates from above. Trees and foliage flourish abundantly around the King, though the blue sky is clouded.

Interpretation: A political or military man, powerful and determined. A professional man with a sharp analytical mind. A person of authority and action who sees facts without emotion. Potent and productive.

Reversed: A revengeful and cruel sadist. Unjustified violence.

The Pentacles

ACE OF PENTACLES

ACE OF PENTACLES

Description: A hand emerges from a cloud holding a shining gold pentacle. On the land below, a path leads from a lush green garden to the mountains and sky beyond. Paths in the Tarot indicate the road to spiritual knowledge. Red roses symbolize perfection and desire. Pure white lilies of abstract thought frame the way. Mountains that represent the intellect and the ascent from earth to heaven are in the background. Clouds mist the area between earth and heaven, making obscure a clear area between the two.

Interpretation: The Ace of Pentacles represents spiritual blessing in the Material World. The path of great wealth and prosperity.

Reversed: Money, material goods are misused. Spiritual poverty.

TWO OF PENTACLES

Description: A youth, wearing two feathers in his hat, tries to balance two pentacles which are contained within the symbol of the harmonious universe . Despite the windy day and choppy waves, a clipper ship manages to stay afloat on the ocean in the background. Ships are a vehicle as the body is a vehicle of the soul.

Interpretation: Effort is required to balance and harmonize career and social affairs during unsteady times. Care is needed in scheduling time and energy.

Reversed: Instability. Changes cause unsteadiness. Too many projects taken on at once prove unprofitable.

THREE OF PENTACLES

Description: A young person begins disciplined work in his artistic craft. He is working with a hammer and chisel on the stone support of a church window. The hammer represents the mysteries of the power of creation. The yellow and red stained glass present three pentacles. The worker is pleased with his progress and concerned with the perfection of his finished product.

Interpretation: Apprenticeship. The sincere effort to develop and utilize one's creative talents and the satisfaction resulting from doing so. Confidence and inner satisfaction.

Reversed: Lack of direction and haphazard attempts show little effort towards goal.

FOUR OF PENTACLES

Description: A well-dressed woman gazes alertly ahead as she stands in front of a solid wall. Walls symbolize that which protects, restricts, and limits. One pentacle is balanced in her crown, meaning it is in the realm of her thoughts. She holds three more pentacles in front. Her crown and rich robe suggest material attainment.

Interpretation: Concentration on money suppresses feelings in other areas. A miserly personality impressed by material gain and standing. This over-developed interest in wealth limits other interests.

Reversed: Loss of money. Dissipation of funds causes anxiety.

FIVE OF PENTACLES

Description: Two miserable figures huddle outside a stained glass church window from which light pours revealing five pentacles. Wrapped in rags, the woman appears chilled as she sorrowfully comforts a battered young man with blood-soaked bandages on his head and hand. He uses a staff to lean upon which indicates his need for spiritual and material support. Blood on bandages refers to the results of intense suffering. Rags symbolize the wounded soul.

Interpretation: Hardships and destitution. The unfortunate couple seek comfort and spiritual guidance from above. A time of confusion and troubles, both emotional and financial.

Reversed: Spiritual and material poverty is lifted.

SIX OF PENTACLES

Description: A man who has rightfully earned his success finds himself in a position to help others. He holds the scales of balance which indicate the control of his money flow. He offers a gold piece to needy hands. Six pentacles are raised in perfect balance behind him.

Interpretation: Good money management and business sense are combined with generosity. These traits put one in the position to help others.

Reversed: Poor money management. Unpaid bills, debts, and loans.

SEVEN OF PENTACLES

Description: A contemplative farmer stands ready with a hoe to reap the benefits of his harvest. A lush garden grows abundantly indicating a productive crop. The plants bear seven pentacles which refer to the financial gain they will harvest. His eyes are looking forward toward the future.

Interpretation: Patience while waiting for well-deserved benefits of labor. Hard work and effort bring financial reward.

Reversed: Unprofitable investments. Wasted energy.

Interpretation: Craftsmanship. Financial gain from the skillful utilization of one's creative abilities. Through past apprenticeships combined with natural talent, thoughts are worked through to creation.

Reversed: Lack of concentration and effort causes second-rate work. Commercialism.

EIGHT OF PENTACLES

Description: A skilled craftsman is laboring with utmost care and attention over a project of his own design. Six pentacles are hung on the wall behind him which represent his accomplishments in his field and the financial reward they have brought. Two pentacles lay on the table, symbolic of continued effort and success. The hammer and chisel refer to the power of creation.

Interpretation: Attainment of financial success and material comforts. Independent enjoyment of luxury and accomplishments in the material plane.

Reversed: Victim of one's wealth. Safety is threatened.

NINE OF PENTACLES

Description: Dressed in lavish robes and adorned with jewels, a woman reaches for grapes which represent abundance. An exotic bird is perched on her finely-gloved hand while nine pentacles form a necklace on her tunic. Her necklace refers to the connecting of the diverse constituent, of success. Her large ring indicates continuity. The pine tree is a symbol of immortality; the pine cone a symbol of fertility.

TEN OF PENTACLES

Description: A wealthy man and woman embrace inside a sturdy stone building. They both wear hats and robes. Outside there are two crossed banners, each bearing five pentacles. Banners symbolize victory and self-assertion.

Interpretation: Financial and family security. A home built on firm foundations.

Reversed: Financial difficulties cause problems in the home.

PAGE OF PENTACLES

Description: A youth, not yet earning a living, gazes thoughtfully upon the land while holding a pentacle. In his cap, which indicates a meditative personality, is a feather. A lake, symbolic of unknown forces, is set under purple mountains. Water that reflects red suggests struggles ahead that must be overcome.

Interpretation: The Page of Pentacles represents a very opinionated youth possessed of high ideals with which to build his future. The Page of Pentacles is serious, scholarly, appreciative of the finer things in life and will not settle for a road that does not lead to these things.

Reversed: Illogical and unrealistic young person.

KNIGHT OF PENTACLES

Description: A proud and stately knight in armor holds his lance high under the autumn sun. The lance is a phallic symbol and also indicates war. The shield he carries is emblazoned with the sign of the pentacle. Oak leaves are bunched together at the top of his helmet. Helmets indicate elevated thought and high ideals.

Interpretation: A diligent person well trained in his field of endeavor. He is capable and dependable. Although interested in science and culture, his ways are materialistic and methodical.

Reversed: Careless, narrowminded and idle person who shows indolence and inertia.

QUEEN OF PENTACLES

Description: A regal queen leans on a pentacle as she gazes across the autumn landscape. She wears fine, heavy robes adorned with a gold piece. Ripened acorns have not yet fallen from the oak's branches. She wears a large ring which indicates continuity.

Interpretation: The Queen of Pentacles is an intelligent, cultured, and elegant woman. Her interests lie in the arts and civic affairs. She is a wealthy woman, financially and emotionally stable. She donates generously to subjects that interest her.

Reversed: A suspicious and narrow-minded woman.

KING OF PENTACLES

Interpretation: A shrewd, established man who has made a success of his business or vocation. A chief of industry, he is intelligent and world-wise. He has a down-to-earth nature, is sensible and protective of those he loves.

Reversed: Corrupt and perverse character not to be trusted.

KING OF PENTACLES

Description: Wearing a helmet decorated with the horns of Taurus, indicating a restless and vital nature, the King of Pentacles looks ahead seriously. The laurel wreath around the helmet indicates victory and success. Ripe grape vines, symbols of fertility and sometimes sacrifice, twine around him. The King firmly holds his scepter with one hand and the pentacle with the other. The gold scepter, symbolizing his authority, is topped with an orb of the world.

Storage of the Cards

The cards must be protected against negative vibrations. Store them wrapped in dark silk in a closed wooden container. Never leave them out in the open or in reach of curious hands.

When you first buy a deck of Tarot cards, examine them carefully to familiarize yourself with them. Be the only one who handles them. The Tarot are powerful psychic images that must be used wisely. When you are through with them, put them away.

It will take a while to get used to the cards, but with serious effort you will begin to understand them and learn how to use them.

Reading the Cards

Reading or divination with the Tarot cards increases awareness and develops intuition. It brings one to a better understanding of one's state in the world at the time of the reading.

To begin a reading, it is important to be in an open, passive state of mind. The relaxed mind is more receptive to the messages the images of the Tarot portray. Gypsies sit with legs uncrossed facing north. One may care to adopt this method.

Examine each card in order to get acquainted with it. Notice the various symbols, colors, and especially the mood of the card in general. After inspecting the cards, shuffle them in a way in which the pictures cannot be seen. Concentrate on filling the cards with your own thoughts, influence, and vibrations. This can take a short time or a long one. When this has been done, divide the cards with the left hand and separate them into three piles to the left. Use the first deck that attracts you for divination. Several methods of reading the cards are listed.

The Ancient Celtic Method of Divination

In the Ancient Celtic Method of Divination as in any other method, the quality of a reading is dependent on the sensitivity and intuitive ability of the Diviner and on his or her growth and perception of the wide range of human experience. Whoever decides to read for another should approach the reading with a respectful spirit and an open mind, as free of personal bias as possible. He or she should always consider the cards relative to the subject's age, sex, and position in life and adapt the meanings thereby. The Ancient Celtic Method of Divination is used for answering a subject's definite question.

The Diviner first selects a card from the suit pertaining to the nature of the question.

Rods—Spiritual matters.
Cups—Emotional matters.
Swords—Power or position.
Pentacles—Monetary matters.

From that suit, the Diviner selects a court card to represent the subject, or the stage he or she is currently in regarding the question. The King is a mature man; the Queen is a mature woman the Knight is a young man; and the Page is a youthful male or female. This card is known as the Significator.

Place the **Significator** face up on the table. Concentrating on the question he wishes to ask, the subject now shuffles the pack thoroughly three times, the faces always downward. Alter shuffling, he cuts the pack into three piles and places them face downward to his left.

The Diviner now picks up the pack from the left, still keeping the cards face downward.

And now begins the Divination.

1.   Turn up the **First Card** and cover the Significator with it and say, "This covers one." This card represents the general atmosphere relevant to the question asked.

2.   Turn up the **Second Card** and lay it across the first, saying, "This crosses one." This card indicates the nature of the forces opposing one, for good or evil.

3.   Turn up the **Third Card** and place it above the Significator, saying, "This crowns one." It represents what the subject hopes for in relation to the question and has not yet been realized but may be in the future.

4.   Turn up the **Fourth Card** and place it below the Significator, saying, "This is beneath one." The card shows the foundation of the matter, that which the subject has already experienced relevant to it.

5.   Turn up the **Fifth Card** and place to the left of the Significator and say, "This is behind one." This card shows the influence that has just passed or is now passing away.

6.   Turn up the **Sixth Card** and place it to the right of the Significator and say, "This is before one." It shows the influence that will operate in the near future.

Now turn up the Seventh, Eighth, Ninth, and Tenth Cards and place one above the other in a line to the right side of the cross.

7.   The **Seventh Card** represents the attitude of the subject toward the matter.

8.   The **Eighth Card** represents the subject's environment and those tendencies or influences in family and friends which may have a bearing on the matter.

9.   The **Ninth Card** indicates the hopes and fears of the subject concerning the matter.

10.   The **Tenth Card** indicates the outcome of the matter, the culmination of all the influences at work in the preceding cards.

The operation is now completed; however, should the Tenth Card indicate an uncertain nature from which no conclusions can be drawn, one can repeat the process using the Tenth Card as Significator. The pack should be shuffled again, cut three times, and the first ten cards taken as before. By this method, a more thorough account of the outcome may be procured.

Should the Tenth Card be a court card, the outcome of the matter may lie in the hand of the person suggested by the card. For further information as to the outcome, one may take the court card in question and use it as Significator and repeat the process again.

In any divination, if the majority of the cards in the layout come from the Major Arcana, the Diviner may deduce that there are powerful forces influencing the subject's affairs either from the outside or from the subject's own unconscious.

Diagram of the Ancient Celtic Method of Divination

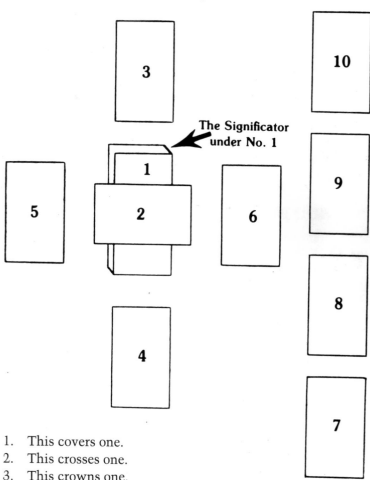

The Significator under No. 1

1. This covers one.
2. This crosses one.
3. This crowns one.
4. This is beneath one.
5. This is behind one.
6. This is before one.
7. Oneself.
8. One's environment—family, friends.
9. One's hopes and fears.
10. The culmination of all preceding influences; the outcome.

Astrological Readings

METHOD I

Obtain a cloth with the twelve houses of the Zodiac drawn upon it in a circular fashion. If you cannot find one in a store, make it yourself. Any material cut into a square large enough to draw the houses of the Zodiac upon will do. The twelve houses of the Zodiac and what they represent are:

Aries	Personality
Taurus	Financial Affairs
Gemini	Brothers, Sisters, Loves
Cancer	Home Life
Leo	Love Affairs
Virgo	Work
Libra	Partnerships
Scorpio	Sex, Birth, Death
Sagittarius	Intellectual Activity
Capricorn	Prestige, Possessions
Aquarius	Social Activities, Groups
Pisces	Emotions, Psyche, Karma

Shuffle the cards and divide them into three groups as explained previously. Starting with the top card from the group chosen, place them in order around the Zodiac starting in the first house of Aries. The meaning of the card will explain your situation in the house it lands in.

METHOD II

The major influence of each month in a new year can be told by what card lands on the corresponding sign.

January	Capricorn	July	Cancer
February	Aquarius	August	Leo
March	Pisces	September	Virgo
April	Aries	October	Libra
May	Taurus	November	Scorpio
June	Gemini	December	Sagittarius

EuRopean Method

The European method of reading cards was popular in Europe around the turn of the century.

Shuffle the cards and pick nine from the deck. Place three to the left; three in the center; and three to the right. The three cards on the left represent important events of the past that lead up to the actions of the present. The three cards in the center represent the present. The three cards on the right represent the future. The cards read across from left to right from the most distant past to the most distant future.

PAST   **PRESENT**   **FUTURE**

Meditation and the Tarot

The only way to meditate is the way in which one personally feels the most comfortable. A quiet area where there will be no distractions or intrusions is important in enabling one to apply total concentration. It doesn't matter upon which card one chooses to begin meditating. It is interesting to note, however, that a card to which one feels attracted may present ideas concerning the stage one is presently experiencing. A card to which one feels no attraction may represent an area that needs development or with which one should cope. There is a reason for one's reaction to every card, including whether or not one finds one Tarot card more appealing than another.

It is the arrangement of universal symbols in the Tarot that generates ideas in the subconscious. Contemplation on the symbols stimulates mental reactions.

Relate one's reactions to the present state of one's mind. Keep an open mind to new ideas or sudden inspirations gained while meditating. Let one's whole being get involved in the meditation.

Imagine one is within the picture on the card, and notice one's reactions. Become absorbed in the mood and vibrations of the experience in order to comprehend the subject fully. Ideas are most valuable at this time, and it is wise to remember them to record later.

Some people feel relaxed after meditating, while others feel excited and eager to pursue their experiences. Of course, for every individual there will be a unique reaction.